Cool
HOLIDAY TREATS

Easy Recipes for Kids to Bake

Pam Price

ABDO
Publishing Company

TO ADULT HELPERS

You're invited to assist up-and-coming pastry chefs in a kitchen near you! And it will pay off in many ways. Your children will develop new skills, gain confidence, and make some delicious treats while learning to bake. What's more, it's going to be a lot of fun.

These recipes are designed to let children bake independently as much as possible. Encourage them to do whatever they are able to do on their own. Also encourage them to try any variations supplied with the recipes and to experiment with their own ideas. Building creativity into the baking process encourages children to think like real chefs.

Before getting started, set some ground rules about using the kitchen, cooking tools, and ingredients. Most important, adult supervision is a must whenever a child uses the oven, stove, or sharp tools.

So put on your aprons and stand by. Let your young bakers take the lead. Watch and learn. Taste their creations. Praise their efforts. Enjoy the culinary adventure!

Visit us at www.abdopublishing.com

Published by ABDO Publishing Company, 8000 West 78th Street, Edina, Minnesota 55439. Copyright © 2010 by Abdo Consulting Group, Inc. International copyrights reserved in all countries. No part of this book may be reproduced in any form without written permission from the publisher. Checkerboard Library™ is a trademark and logo of ABDO Publishing Company.

Printed in the United States of America, North Mankato, Minnesota
092009
012010

PRINTED ON RECYCLED PAPER

Editor: Liz Salzmann
Series Concept: Nancy Tuminelly
Cover and Interior Design: Anders Hanson, Mighty Media, Inc.
Photo Credits: Anders Hanson, Shutterstock

The following manufacturers/names appearing in this book are trademarks: Bialetti®, C&H®, KitchenAid®, Kraft®, McCormick®, Morton®, Proctor Silex®

Library of Congress Cataloging-in-Publication Data

Price, Pamela S.
   Cool holiday treats : easy recipes for kids to bake / Pam Price.
      p. cm. -- (Cool baking)
   Includes index.
   ISBN 978-1-60453-776-5
   1. Holiday cookery--Juvenile literature. I. Title.
   TX739.P75 2010
   641.5'68--dc22
                                    2009029858

Table of Contents

Baking Is Cool

Baking traditional treats is a great way to celebrate holidays!

A tradition is a thought, action, or behavior that passes from one generation to the next. We often do traditional things at holidays. These traditions might be part of our religious beliefs. Or they might just be things our families have "always done."

Food is often an important part of our traditions. There are certain foods that we prepare or eat only on that holiday. Sometimes the food is **symbolic**. Sometimes a food becomes part of the holiday because that is when it is available. In some states, strawberry shortcake is popular on the Fourth of July. This is because strawberries are ripe in early July.

This book includes desserts for celebrating holidays throughout the year. You probably already have traditions for holidays and other occasions. This book may include holidays that you don't celebrate. Or it might offer a new food for a holiday you do celebrate.

Perhaps your baking will start a new tradition in your family. How fun is that!

GET THE PICTURE!

When a step number in a recipe has a colored circle around it, look for the picture that goes with it. The circle around the photo will be the same color as the step number.

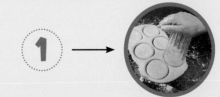

1 →

Ready, Set, Bake!

Preparation is a key element of successful baking.
Here are some things to keep in mind.

ASK PERMISSION

> Get permission to use the kitchen, baking tools, and ingredients.

> If you'd like to do something by yourself, say so. As long as you can do it safely, do it!

> Ask for help when you need it. Professional chefs have *sous chefs*, which means "assistant chefs" in French. You can have one too!

BE PREPARED

Read the whole recipe the day before you plan to bake.

> Make sure you have all the ingredients. Do you need to go to the grocery store?

> Will there be enough time? Sometimes dough needs to chill before you form it into a crust or cookies.

When it's time to bake, these steps will help you be organized.

> Gather all the tools and equipment you will need.

> Prepare the pans as directed and preheat the oven.

> Gather the listed ingredients. Sometimes you need prepared ingredients such as chopped nuts or sifted flour. Do those prep jobs as you gather the ingredients.

> Finally, do the recipe steps in the order they are listed.

Safety First!

When you bake you need to use an oven. Sometimes you also have to use sharp tools. Ask an adult helper to be in the kitchen with you. Here's how to keep it safe.

HOT STUFF

> Set up a cooling rack ahead of time.

> Make sure it's easy to get from the oven to the cooling area. There should be no people or things in the way.

> Always use oven mitts, not towels, when handling hot pots and pans.

> The oven is hot too. Don't bump into the racks or the door.

THAT'S SHARP

> Choose a small knife. Cut just a small amount of food at a time.

> Always keep your other hand away from the blade.

> Work slowly and keep your eyes on the knife.

KEY SYMBOLS

In this book, you will see some symbols beside the recipes. Here is what they mean.

SUPER SHARP!
You need to use a knife for this recipe. Ask an adult to stand by.

SUPER COOL!
This symbol means there are other ways to make the recipe.

Germ Alert!

It's so tempting, but you shouldn't eat raw dough that contains eggs. Raw eggs may contain salmonella **bacteria**, which can cause food poisoning. Eating raw cookie dough that contains eggs might make you sick. Really sick! Ask an adult if it's okay to lick bowls, beaters, and spoons.

KEEP IT CLEAN

> Tie back long hair.

> Wash your hands before you begin baking. Rub them with soap for 20 seconds before rinsing. Wash them again if you eat, sneeze, cough, take a bathroom break, or touch the trash container.

> Use clean tools and equipment. If you lick a spoon, wash it before using it again.

> Make sure that your cutting board hasn't had raw meat on it.

Tools of the Trade

These are the basic tools used for baking holiday treats.
Each recipe in this book lists the tools you will need.

MEASURING CUPS

MEASURING SPOONS

MIXING BOWLS

PASTRY BLENDER

ROLLING PIN

SMALL SAUCEPAN

FROSTING SPATULA

WHISK

MIXER AND BEATERS

ZESTER

SILICONE SPATULA

SERRATED KNIFE

WOODEN SPOON

KNIFE AND CUTTING BOARD

**PIG-SHAPED
COOKIE CUTTER**

**4-INCH
BISCUIT CUTTER**

COOKIE SHEET

BAKING SHEET

9 × 13-INCH BAKING DISH

8-INCH ROUND CAKE PAN

9-INCH SPRINGFORM PAN

SMALL U.S. FLAGS

8 × 8-INCH CAKE PAN

OVEN MITTS

PLASTIC WRAP

WAXED PAPER

SPATULA

COOLING RACK

TOOTHPICKS

Cool Ingredients

Butter, flour, sugar. You can make many different goodies based on these three ingredients! Add a few others, and the possibilities are endless.

BUTTER

Always choose unsalted butter for baking. You add salt in most recipes. Using unsalted butter keeps the dough from having too much salt.

FLOUR

In a recipe, the word *flour* means all-purpose wheat flour. But other grains can be ground into flour too. Some of these grains include kamut, rye, buckwheat, and corn.

SUGAR

You use several types of sugar for baking. Most common are granulated sugar, powdered sugar, and brown sugar. Sometimes a recipe may call for corn syrup, molasses, or honey. If a recipe just says *sugar*, it means granulated sugar.

About Organics

Organic foods are grown without **synthetic** fertilizers and **pesticides**. This is good for the earth. And, recent studies show that organic foods may be more nutritious than **conventionally** grown foods.

Organic foods used to be hard to find. But now you can find organic versions of most foods. Organic foods are more expensive than conventionally grown foods. Families must decide for themselves whether to spend extra for organic foods.

EGGS

Eggs come in many sizes. Use large eggs unless the recipe says otherwise. Bring eggs to room temperature before you add them to the dough.

BAKING SODA AND BAKING POWDER

Baking soda and baking powder are common **leavening** agents. Leavening agents are ingredients that make baked goods rise.

MILK AND CREAM

You can usually use whatever milk you have, whether it is skim, low fat, or whole milk. Substituting usually won't noticeably affect the quality of what you're making. However, use cream if a recipe says to. You can make buttermilk if you don't have any. Put one tablespoon of white vinegar in a measuring cup. Then and add milk until you have one cup of liquid.

SALT

You may be surprised to see salt in a dessert recipe. Salt is a flavor **enhancer**. It enhances the flavors in your baked goods, whether they are sweet or **savory**.

THICKENERS

When you make a crisp with juicy fresh fruit, you need to use a thickener. Otherwise, all that juice makes a soupy mess! Common thickeners for crisps are **tapioca** powder or flakes, cornstarch, and flour.

EXTRACTS

There are many flavoring **extracts** used in baking. Some of these are vanilla, lemon, and maple. You will probably use vanilla extract most often. Vanilla extract is made from the beans, or seedpods, of tropical orchids.

CHOCOLATE

Chocolate comes from the bean of the cacao tree. When cocoa beans are processed, the cocoa particles and the cocoa butter are separated. Then they are recombined in different **formulas** such as semisweet, bittersweet, and milk chocolate. In general, the higher the cocoa content, the stronger the taste.

FRUIT

You çan use almost any fresh fruit to make a crisp. Popular choices include apples, pears, peaches, nectarines, rhubarb, and strawberries. Choose fruit that is ripe and not bruised. If you use frozen fruit, be sure to thaw it first.

Sometimes recipes also call for citrus zest. The zest is the colored part of the citrus fruit's skin. The oils in the skins are very flavorful, so little zest adds goes a long way!

NUTS

Nuts, usually walnuts or pecans, add flavor to baked goods. Luckily, you can buy them already sliced or chopped!

Allergy Alert

Millions of people have food allergies or food intolerance. Foods that most often cause allergic reactions include milk, eggs, peanuts, tree nuts, and wheat. Common food intolerances include lactose and gluten. Lactose is the sugar in milk. Gluten is the protein in wheat.

Baked goods can be a real hazard for people with food allergies or intolerances. If a friend cannot eat the goodies you're offering, don't be offended. It could be a life or death matter for your friend.

Cool Techniques

These are the techniques that bakers use. If you can't remember how to do something, just reread these pages.

MEASURING DRY INGREDIENTS

Dip the measuring spoon or measuring cup into whatever you're measuring. Use a butter knife to scrape off the excess.

MIXING DRY INGREDIENTS

Unless the recipe says otherwise, always stir the dry ingredients together first. Measure them into a bowl and stir them with a fork or a whisk.

CREAMING

Creaming means beating something until it is smooth and creamy. Butter is often creamed before it is used in a recipe. Unless the recipe says otherwise, use butter that is near room temperature.

CUTTING IN

Cutting in means working butter into flour until the mixture is crumbly. Use a pastry blender, a fork, or your fingertips.

SEPARATING AN EGG

Rap the egg firmly on the countertop. Hold the egg over a bowl and pull the shell apart. Gently pass the egg back and forth between the pieces of shell. The white will fall into the bowl. The yolk will remain in the shell.

WHIPPING CREAM

Pour the whipping cream into a chilled bowl with deep sides. Beat on high speed until the cream forms peaks. Don't overbeat, or you will make butter!

SCRAPING A BOWL

When using a mixer, turn off the mixer occasionally and scrape the sides. Then scrape the bottom of the bowl with a silicone spatula. That way you'll be sure that all of the ingredients are completely mixed. Recipes don't usually mention this important step. You just have to remember to do it!

GREASING A PAN

Butter wrappers are great for greasing pans. If you don't have one, use waxed paper and a bit of butter. Run the paper and butter all around the inside of the pan. There should be a light coating of butter on the bottom and sides.

FLOURING A PAN

Sometimes you will need to flour the pan after you grease it. Sprinkle about a tablespoon of flour in the greased pan. Hold the pan with one hand over the sink. Tap its side firmly with the other hand. As you tap, twist and turn the pan to move the flour around. When all the surfaces are lightly coated, dump out the extra flour.

ROLLING OUT DOUGH

Shape the dough into a disc. Place it on a floured countertop or pastry cloth. Roll the dough in one direction. Turn the dough or the rolling pin and roll in another direction. Continue rolling in different directions until the dough is the right thickness.

ZESTING CITRUS FRUIT

Gently scrape the fruit over the small holes of a grater or citrus zester. Just remove the colored part of the skin. Then chop the zest with a small knife. The pieces should be no longer than ¼ inch.

I ❤ You Cake

Celebrate Valentine's Day with a cake that says it all!

MAKES 10–12 SERVINGS

TOOLS:

8-inch round cake pan
8 x 8-inch cake pan
measuring cups

measuring spoons
mixing bowls
whisk

mixer and beaters
silicone spatula
toothpick

cooling rack
oven mitts
serving platter

waxed paper
frosting spatula or butter knife

TO MAKE THE CAKE

1 Preheat the oven to 350 degrees. Grease and flour the cake pans and set them aside.

2 In a small bowl, whisk together the flour, baking powder, and salt. Set the bowl aside.

3 Put the butter and sugar in another bowl. Beat until the mixture is light and fluffy. This will take about 3 minutes. Add the eggs one at a time, beating after you add each one. Add the vanilla and beat for about another 5 minutes.

4 Add about a third of the flour mixture and a third of the milk. Beat on low speed just until the flour is mixed in. Add another third of the flour and another third of the milk. Beat just until mixed. Add the remaining flour and milk and beat just until mixed.

5 Pour the batter into the prepared cake pans. Bake for about 20 to 25 minutes. The cake is done when a toothpick **inserted** in the center comes out clean. Place the pans on a cooling rack for 5 minutes. Then turn the pans over to remove the cakes. Let the cakes cool completely. Make the frosting while they are cooling (see next page).

TO MAKE THE FROSTING

1 Cream the butter until it is light and fluffy.

2 Add one-fourth of the powdered sugar and one-fourth of the milk. Starting with the mixer on low speed, beat until smooth.

3 Continue beating in small amounts of milk and powdered sugar. When you add powdered sugar, start beating on low. Then increase the mixer speed.

4 When the frosting is spreadable, don't add any more milk. Note that you may not need to use all of the milk.

5 Beat in the vanilla and the red food coloring. Use just enough food coloring to tint the frosting pink or red.

TO FINISH THE CAKE

1 Cut the round cake in half. Place the halves against two sides of the square cake to make a heart.

2 Tuck strips of waxed paper under the edges of the cake. Use a butter knife or a small frosting spatula to frost the cake.

3 Remove the waxed paper. Top the cake with small heart decorations or pink, red, and white sprinkles.

18

Strawberry Shortcake

MAKES 6 SERVINGS

Show your patriotic colors on the Fourth of July!

INGREDIENTS

FOR THE CAKE

2 cups flour

¼ cup sugar

2 teaspoons baking powder

1 teaspoon salt

⅓ cup cold butter, cut into small pieces

¾ cup milk

FOR THE FRUIT

1 pint strawberries, cleaned and cut in half

1 pint blueberries, cleaned and drained

1 tablespoon sugar

FOR THE WHIPPED CREAM

1 cup whipping cream

1 tablespoon sugar

TOOLS:

measuring cups
measuring spoons
mixing bowls
whisk

pastry blender
fork
rolling pin
4-inch biscuit cutter

baking sheet
cooling rack
oven mitts
silicone spatula

serrated knife
mixer and beaters
spoon
dessert plates

small U.S. flag picks

1 Preheat the oven to 450 degrees.

2 Whisk together the flour, sugar, baking powder, and salt. Use your fingertips or a pastry blender to cut in the butter. Stop when the mixture looks like coarse crumbs.

3 Use a fork to stir in the milk. Stop stirring when the dough forms a ball.

4 Place the dough on a lightly floured countertop. **Knead** it for about 1 minute until it is smooth.

5 Roll out the dough to form a ½-inch thick rectangle. Use the biscuit cutter or a large drinking glass to cut out six circles. Place them on an ungreased baking sheet. Bake for about 10 minutes or until they are lightly browned.

6 Place the shortcakes on a cooling rack. When they are cool, slice each one in half crosswise.

7 Put the strawberry halves and blueberries in a bowl. Add 1 tablespoon of sugar. Stir to coat the fruit with the sugar. Set this bowl aside.

8 Make the whipped cream right before you are ready to serve the shortcakes. Place the whipping cream and the sugar in a mixing bowl. Beat the cream until it forms stiff peaks. Do not overbeat or you will make butter!

9 Place the bottom half of a shortcake on a dessert plate. Place a spoonful of whipped cream on the shortcake. Top the whipped cream with a spoonful of fruit. Place the top half of the shortcake over the fruit. Top with a small dollop of whipped cream and a small U.S. flag.

Honey Nut Passover Cake

This cake is perfect for Passover because it has no flour!

INGREDIENTS

FOR THE CAKE

- ½ cup matzoh meal
- ½ teaspoon cinnamon
- ¼ teaspoon salt
- ¾ cup sugar
- ¼ cup packed brown sugar
- ¼ cup vegetable oil
- 3 eggs
- 3 tablespoons orange juice
- ½ cup finely chopped almonds
- 1 cup finely chopped walnuts

FOR THE SYRUP

- ⅔ cup sugar
- ¼ cup honey
- ⅓ cup orange juice
- 1 tablespoon lemon juice
- ¼ cup water
- ¼ teaspoon cinnamon

TOOLS:

8 x 8-inch cake pan	measuring spoons	whisk	cooling rack	fork
measuring cups	mixing bowls	wooden spoon	oven mitts	small saucepan

1 Preheat the oven to 350 degrees. Grease an 8 x 8-inch cake pan.

2 Whisk together the matzoh meal, cinnamon, and salt. Set this bowl aside.

 Whisk together the sugar, brown sugar, vegetable oil, eggs, and orange juice.

 Stir the matzoh mixture into the egg mixture. Then stir in the chopped almonds and chopped walnuts.

5 Pour the batter into the prepared pan. Bake for 35 to 40 minutes. The top will be light brown and firm. Place the pan on a cooling rack and let the cake cool completely.

6 While the cake cools, make the syrup. Place the sugar, honey, orange juice, lemon juice, water, and cinnamon in a small saucepan. Simmer the mixture, stirring it occasionally. Let it simmer until it is syrupy and all the sugar has dissolved. This takes about 10 minutes. Take the pan off the heat and let the syrup cool.

 Use a fork to poke holes all over the top of the cake. Slowly pour the cooled syrup over the top of the cake. The syrup should soak into the cake, not run off. If it runs off, pour more slowly or poke more holes in the cake.

 Refrigerate the cake for at least 4 hours before cutting it. This cake is very sweet, so cut small pieces!

Memorable Rhubarb Crisp

Rhubarb makes a great Memorial Day dessert!

MAKES 10–12 SERVINGS

TOOLS: 9 × 13-inch baking dish · small knife · cutting board · measuring cups · measuring spoons · mixing bowls · wooden spoon · pastry blender · cooling rack · oven mitts

1 Preheat the oven to 375 degrees.

2 Combine the chopped rhubarb, apple slices, sugar, **tapioca** flakes, and cinnamon in a bowl. Stir until the fruit is evenly coated with the dry ingredients. Pour it into the baking dish.

3 To make the topping, combine the butter, ¾ cup flour, cinnamon, brown sugar, and nutmeg in a bowl. Use your fingertips or a pastry blender to cut the butter into the dry ingredients. When the mixture is crumbly, stir in the oats and nuts.

4 Sprinkle the topping evenly over the fruit. Bake the crisp for about an hour. It is done when the topping is browned and the juices are bubbling up. Put it on a cooling rack until the pan is cool enough to handle. Serve warm.

Super Cool!

You can make a crisp with almost any fruit. Use this recipe, but substitute apples, pears, or peaches for the rhubarb. Or, mix berries and peaches.

Festive Apple Kuchen

Celebrate Labor Day with this delicious treat!

MAKES 10 SERVINGS

INGREDIENTS

FOR THE CRUST

1 cup flour

¼ teaspoon salt

¼ teaspoon cinnamon

⅓ cup butter, cut into small pieces

¼ cup sour cream

FOR THE TOPPING

3 cups apples, peeled, cored, and sliced

½ cup sour cream

3 egg yolks

1 cup sugar

¼ cup flour

1 teaspoon vanilla

TOOLS: 9-inch springform pan   mixing bowls   pastry blender   oven mitts
measuring cups   knife   wooden spoon
measuring spoons   whisk   cooling rack

1 Preheat the oven to 350 degrees. Grease the pan and set it aside.

2 Put the flour, salt, and cinnamon in a bowl and whisk them together. Add the butter. Cut it into the flour with your fingertips or a pastry blender. When the mixture looks like small crumbs, stir in the ¼ cup of sour cream.

3 Press the mixture evenly over the bottom of the pan. Bake the crust about 20 to 25 minutes, or until it is lightly browned. Put the pan on a cooling rack and let it cool slightly.

4 For the topping, arrange the apple slices on the crust.

5 Whisk together the sour cream, egg yolks, sugar, flour, and vanilla. Pour this mixture over the apples.

6 Bake the **kuchen** for about 45 minutes. Test the kuchen for doneness. When a knife tip **inserted** into the center comes out clean, it is done.

7 Put the pan on a cooling rack until it is cool enough to handle. Release the clasp on the side of the pan and lift it off. You can leave the kuchen on the bottom of the pan.

Christmas Cochinitos

These "little pigs" are traditional Mexican Christmas cookies!

MAKES ABOUT 3 DOZEN COOKIES

INGREDIENTS

- 2¼ cups flour
- ½ teaspoon baking powder
- ½ teaspoon baking soda
- ¾ cup butter
- ½ cup packed brown sugar
- ½ cup corn syrup
- 1 teaspoon vanilla extract
- zest of 1 orange, finely grated
- 1 teaspoon cinnamon

TOPPING

- 2 tablespoons sugar
- 1 teaspoon cinnamon

TOOLS:

measuring cups	whisk	silicone spatula	rolling pin	cooling rack
measuring spoons	zester or grater	plastic wrap	pig-shaped cookie	oven mitts
mixing bowls	mixer and beaters	cookie sheets	cutter	spatula

1 Whisk together the flour, baking powder, and baking soda in a bowl.

2 In a separate bowl, cream the butter until it is light and fluffy. Beat in the brown sugar, corn syrup, vanilla, orange zest, and cinnamon.

3 Add the flour mixture in thirds. Stir well after each addition. Form the dough into two balls. Wrap them in plastic wrap. Refrigerate them for about 2 hours.

4 Preheat the oven to 375 degrees. Grease the cookie sheets.

5 Lightly flour the countertop and place one ball of dough on it. Roll out the dough until it is ¼-inch thick. Cut out cookies with a pig-shaped cookie cutter. Place the cookies on a cookie sheet. Gather the scraps and set them aside.

6 Roll out the other ball of dough and cut out more cookies. Combine the scraps from both balls. Roll them out to make more cookies. Keep rolling out the scraps and cutting cookies until all the dough is used.

7 When you are ready to bake the cookies, stir together the sugar and cinnamon to make the topping. Sprinkle a light dusting of cinnamon-sugar over the cookies. Bake for about 10 minutes or until the cookies are light brown. Let the cookies cool on the cookie sheet for about 3 minutes. Then use a spatula to move them to a cooling rack.

Wrap It Up!

Baking holiday treats is a fun way to experience our traditions!

Longstanding traditions are those that our families have done for generations. Often we have traditions for important personal, cultural, and religious holidays. There are many ways to celebrate birthdays, Thanksgiving, Christmas, Hanukkah, and other occasions.

You can also make new traditions or borrow traditions from other places. You can pick any holiday and create a tradition for it. The recipes in this book can help you get started!

Part of the fun of a new tradition is sharing it. Invite your friends to share the treats you baked. Holidays are a great time to give treats to your friends and family. Better yet, invite them to help you bake. That can become a tradition too!

Glossary

bacteria – tiny, one-celled organisms that can only be seen through a microscope.

conventional – in the usual way.

enhance – to increase or improve.

extract – a product made by concentrating the juices taken from something such as a plant.

formula – a combination of specific amounts of different ingredients or elements.

insert – to put something into something else.

knead – to press, fold, and stretch something, such as dough.

kuchen – German for "cake."

leavening – a substance such as yeast or baking soda that makes baked goods rise.

pesticide – a substance used to kill insects.

savory – tasty and flavorful but not sweet.

symbolic – representing something else.

synthetic – produced artificially through chemistry.

tapioca – a food made from the starchy root of the tropical cassava plant.

To learn more about cool baking, visit ABDO Publishing Company on the World Wide Web at **www.abdopublishing.com.** Web sites about cool baking are featured on our Book Links page. These links are routinely monitored and updated to provide the most current information available.

Index